RED

BOCK'S GREATEST GOSPEL HITS

INDEX

Fred Bock Music Company

FRED BOCK'S FOREWORD

Whenever I go to a record store, I always find scads of records like, "The Best of Frank Sinatra," or "The Best of Ethel Smith," or "The Best of The Krell-tones." And now, the day I have *longed for* has arrived: FRED BOCK'S GREATEST HITS for All Organs . . ."The Best of Fred Bock" is here! So here we go; a new book, and a new foreword. These selections have been favorites in the thirty or so organ books I have written, and I am thrilled to have this book of winners all together *under one roof.*

An interesting addition this time is a complete listing of every single Fred Bock organ arrangement in print. Compiling that list and organizing it was a big job; but thanks to my secretary, Susie Cole, the job (for me) was a breeze! Also, if you run across a few titles in that listing you don't know, you can easily locate the collection and publisher.

If you would like to know about new books and records I do from time to time, drop me a note. I'll be happy to put you on my mailing list so you will know the moment a new organ book is hot off the press. My address is Box 333, Tarzana, CA 91356.

On page 5 starts the music and it continues for 144 pages. I predict that you will have a good time with these 43 selections . . . hymns, gospel songs, fol songs and spirituals: the variety is wide! I am esp cially pleased to include the popular Stuart Hambl songs: *Until Then, This Ole House, How Big Is Go The Lord Is Counting on You,* and *Teach Me, Lor to Wait.* We also have songs by leading composers su as John Peterson, Bill Gaither, Andrae Crouch ar Otis Skillings – and ever-popular selections such *The Old Rugged Cross, Beyond the Sunset, Th Longer I Serve Him, I Just Feel Like Something Goo is About To Happen, In the Garden, It Took a Mirac* – and some popular oldies like *Amazing Grace, Just Closer Walk With Thee, Blessed Assurance,* and *He Got the Whole World in His Hands.*

My wish is that you will really enjoy this book ar find it to be useful, refreshing, and rewarding. And hope, too, that when you play these arrangement those who listen will like them. That would mal both you and I feel great! Happy playing.

FRED BOCK
June, 1978

COMPLETE LISTING OF FRED BOCK ORGAN ARRANGEMENTS

(10)	A Symphony of Song
(26)	A Touch of Latin
(11)	A Wedding Prayer
(11)	Abide With Me
(13)	Alfie
(18)	Alma Mater No. 1 (Far Above Cayuga's Waters)
(18)	Alma Mater No. 2 (O Tannenbaum)
(23)	All God's Children
(24)	All Hail the Power of Jesus' Name
(16)	All He Wants Is You
(1/7)	Alleluia!
(13/20)	Alley Cat
(19)	Am I A Soldier of the Cross? (Meditation On *Arlington*)
(17)	Amazing Grace
(27)	Amen!
(18)	America (My Country 'Tis of Thee)
(18)	America, Our Heritage
(18)	America, the Beautiful
(19/25)	Angels, From the Realms of Glory (Meditation On *Zegent Square*)
(25)	Angels, We Have Heard On High
(11)	At This Altar
(20)	Autumn Leaves
(18)	Battle Humn Of The Republic
(11)	Because
(1/5)	Because He Lives
(1/5)	Bethlehem, Galilee, Gethsemane
(10)	Beyond the Sunset
(5)	Blackwoods (Jazz solo, published by Gentry Publications)
(7)	Bless This House
(3)	Blessed Assurance
(28)	Born Again
(11)	Bridal Chorus
(24)	Christ Is Made the Sure Foundation
(24)	Come, Christians, Join and Sing
(14)	Come, Holy Spirit
(18/24)	Come Thou Almighty King
(13)	Count Every Star
(20)	Danke Schoen
(3)	Day By Day
(28)	Do It Right This Time
(17)	Don't Go Away Without Jesus
(21)	Don't Send Those Kids to Sunday School
(13)	Don't Take It So Hard
(27)	Down By the Riverside
(13)	Dreams of the Everyday Housewife
(11)	Each For the Other
(6/23)	Even So, Lord Jesus Come
(15)	Every Time I Feel The Spirit
(18)	Finlandia (Sibelius)
(24)	For the Beauty of the Earth
(18)	Gaudeamus Igitur
(14)	Gentle Shepherd
(1/5)	Get All Excited
(2)	Give My Regards To Broadway
(27)	Go Tell It On the Mountain
(1/6)	God Gave the Song/Redeeming Love
(10)	God Is So Wonderful

PUBLISHER DIRECTORY

1. **ALLELUIA! Organ Book**
Benson Publishing Company, 365 Great Circle Rd., Nashville, TN 37228
2. **BROADWAY'S BEST BALLADS**
Gentry Publications, Theodore Presser Company, Bryn Mawr, PA 19010
3. **CRUSADE FAVORITES FROM AROUND THE WORLD**
Word, Inc., P.O. Box 1790, Waco, TX 76703
4. **4 HYMNS FOR THE ORGAN**
Fred Bock Music Co., Alexandria House, Box 300, Alexandria, IN 46001
5. **GET ALL EXCITED Organ Book**
Gaither Music Company, Alexandria House, Box 300, Alexandria, IN 46001
6. **HE TOUCHED ME Organ Book**
Gaither Music Company, Alexandria House, Box 300, Alexandria, IN 46001
7. **HE'S EVERYTHING TO ME Organ Book**
Fred Bock Music Co., Alexandria House, Box 300, Alexandria, IN 46001
8. **HIS NAME IS WONDERFUL Organ Book**
Manna Music, Inc., 2111 Kenmere, Burbank, CA 91504
9. **HOW GREAT THOU ART Organ Book**
Manna Music, Inc., 2111 Kenmere, Burbank, CA 91504
10. **HOW GREAT THOU ART Organ Book**
Word, Inc., P.O. Box 1790, Waco, TX 76703
11. **IT'S WEDDING TIME**
Singspiration, Inc., 4145 Kalamazoo Ave., S.E., Grand Rapids, MI 49508
12. **JOHN W. PETERSON Organ Book**
Singspiration, Inc., 4145 Kalamazoo Ave., S.E., Grand Rapids, MI 49508
13. **LATEST HOT FOURTEEN ORGAN SOLOS**
Charles Hansen Publications, 1842 W. Avenue, Miami Beach, FL 33139
14. **LET'S JUST PRAISE THE LORD Organ Book**
Gaither Music Company, Alexandria House, Box 300, Alexandria, IN 46001
15. **MORE GOSPEL SONGS FOR ALL ORGANS**
Word, Inc., P.O. Box 1790, Waco, TX 76703
16. **MUSIC FOR ORGAN: WITH A LITTLE HELP FROM MY FRIENDS**
Manna Music, Inc., 2111 Kenmere, Burbank, CA 91504
17. **MY GOD AND I Organ Book**
Fred Bock Music Co., Alexandria House, Box 300, Alexandria, IN 46001
18. **ORGAN MUSIC FOR CEREMONIAL OCCASIONS**
Shawnee Press, Inc., Delaware Water Gap, PA 18327
19. **ORGAN SOUNDS FOR WORSHIP**
Lorenz Industries, 501 E. Third, Dayton OH 45401
20. **SUPERIOR SOLOS BY BOCK**
Charles Hansen Publications. 1842 W. Avenue, Miami Beach, FL 33139
21. **STUART HAMBLEN'S GOSPEL SONGS Arranged for All Organs**
Hamblen Music Company, Alexandria House, Box 300, Alexandria, IN 46001
22. **TELL THE WORLD Organ Book**
Fred Bock Music Co., Alexandria House, Box 300, Alexandria, IN 46001
23. **THE KING IS COMING Organ Book**
Benson Publishing Company, 365 Great Circle Rd., Nashville, TN 37228
24. **VARIANTS ON HYMNTUNES FOR CONGREGATIONAL SINGING**
Fred Bock Music Co., Alexandria House, Box 300, Alexandria, IN 46001
25. **VARIATIONS ON CHRISTMAS MELODIES**
Lillenas Publishing Company, P.O. Box 527, Kansas City, MO 64141
26. **VARIETY SHOWCASE**
Gentry Publications, Theodore Presser Company, Bryn Mawr, PA 19010
27. **WADE IN THE WATER**
Word, Inc., P.O. Box 1790, Waco, TX 76703
28. **YOUNG WORLD ORGANIST**
Lillenas Publishing Company, P.O. Box 527, Kansas City, MO 64141

HOW BIG IS GOD

HAMMOND	SPINET	OTHERS
Upper: 00 8080 600 Full Vibrato	Upper: 00 8080 600 Full Vibrato	Upper: Clarinet 8' Full Vibrato
Lower: F♯ Full Vibrato	Lower: 5533 2200 Full Vibrato	Lower: Strings 8' Full Vibrato
Pedal: 44	Pedal: 4	Pedal: Bourdon 16'

STUART HAMBLEN
Arr. by Fred Bock

room so small with-in my Mas-ter's house The o-pen
sky but a por-tion of His yard. How Bis Is God! How
In light rhythm
big and wide His vast do-main, To try to tell these
lips can on-ly start, He's big e-nough to

rule His might - y un - i - verse, Yet small e - nough to
live with - in the heart.
A little faster
f

TO GOD BE THE GLORY

HAMMOND
Lower 02 7808 447, or [G]
Ped. 45 Vibrato off
Vibrato off

Lower Full (*ff*)
Ensemble 8', 4', 2'
Ped. Flutes, Diapason 8'
Light 16' if not too heavy.
Vibrato off

Words & Music by
Fanny Crosby
William Doane
Arranged by Fred Bock

Briskly, with a baroque feel

tone-ment for sin. And o-pened the life-gate that all may go in. Praise the Lord! Praise the
Lord! Let the earth hear His voice. Praise the Lord! Praise the Lord! Let the peo-ple re -
joice! O come to the Fa-ther through Je-sus the Son. And give Him the
glo-ry, great things He hath done!
1
2
Slower

HAPPINESS IS THE LORD

HAMMOND
Upper A# 77 5528 224
Lower A# 00 5615 211
Ped. 53
Full Vibrato

OTHERS
Upper Flutes 16', 8', 5⅓', 4', 2'
Lower Flutes and Strings 8', 4'
Ped. Flutes 16', 8'
Full Vibrato

Words & Music by
Ira Stanphill
Arranged by Fred Bock

Hap-pi-ness is a new cre - a - tion, "Je-sus and me," in
close re - la - tion, Hav-ing a part in His sal-va-tion, Hap-pi-ness is the Lord.
f
Real joy is mine, No mat-ter if the tear-drops
Lower
start; I've found the se - cret, It's Je - sus in my heart!

Upper
Hap-pi-ness is to be for-giv-en, Liv-ing a life that's
worth the liv-ing, tak-ing a trip that leads to heav-en,
Hap-pi-ness is the Lord.
Lower f

Upper
8va
rit.
ff
ff

I BELIEVE IN MIRACLES

HAMMOND	SPINET	OTHERS
(U) – 00 8808 000	(U) – 00 8808 000	(U) – Flutes 8′-4′-2
[L] – [F♯] or [E]	[L] – 4433 0000	[L] – Soft Strings 8′-4′, Soft Flute 8′
Ped.– 42	Ped.– 3	Ped.– Soft Flute 16′
Full Vibrato	Full Vibrato	Full Vibrato

JOHN W. PETERSON
Arr. by Fred Bock

ten.
ten.
U with very light feel of rhythm
L

accel.
L
f
U
broadly
L
mp
L

THE LONGER I SERVE HIM

HAMMOND	SPINET	OTHERS
Upper: 00 7817 224 Full Vibrato	Upper: 00 7817 224 Full Vibrato	Upper: Tibia 8' 4' 2' Salicional 8', Full Vibrato
Lower: 00 5523 200 Full Vibrato	Lower: 5523 2000 Full Vibrato	Lower: Flutes 8' Full Vibrato
Pedal: 42	Pedal: 4	Pedal: Tibia 16'

Words and Music by
WILLIAM J. GAITHER
Arr. by Fred Bock

love Him, more love He be - stows. Each day is like
heav - en, my heart o - ver - flows, THE LONG - ER I
SERVE HIM the sweet - er He grows.
Smoothly
L
Since I
start - ed for the king - dom, since my

life He con - trols
Since I
gave my heart to Je - sus, The Long - er I
Serve Him the sweet - er He grows.
U
f

mf
U
mp
Slowly
pp

HIS EYE IS ON THE SPARROW

For General Electronic or Pipe Organs

Upper: Flutes 16', 4', 2'
Lower: Viola (Strings) 8'
Pedal: 16', 8', Medium

For Pre-Set Organs

(A#) 70 0615 000
[A#] 00 5424 110
Pedal 5-2
Vibrato 3

For Spinet Drawbar Organs

(U) 70 0615 000
[L] 5424 1100
Pedal 3-Fast Decay
Vibrato On, Normal

CHARLES GABRIEL
Arranged by Fred Bock

Meditatively, with motion

eye is on the sparrow And I know He watch-es me. His eye is on the
Faster
spar-row And I know He watches me. I sing be-cause I'm hap-py. I
As before
sing be-cause I'm free For His eye is on the spar-row L And I
ad lib.
ten. ten.
r. h.
know He watch-es me.
mp
l. h.
ten. ten.
pp

UNTIL THEN

HAMMOND	SPINET	OTHERS
Upper: 00 8888 000 Full Vibrato	Upper: 00 8888 000 Full Vibrato	Upper: Strings & Flutes 8',4',2' Full Vibrato
Lower: F Full Vibrato	Lower: 4533 2201 Full Vibrato	Lower: Strings 8', 4' Full Vibrato
Pedal: 54	Pedal: 5	Pedal: Bourdon 16', Flute 8'

STUART HAMBLEN
Arr. by Fred Bock

mem - ber, A heart - ache here is but a step - ping
stone. A - long a trail that's wind - ing al - ways
ten.
ten.
up - ward, This trou - bled world is
U Add 16'
8va
U not my fi - nal home. But Un - til
3
3

8
ten.
Then, my heart will go on singing, Until
ten.
ten.
8
Off 16'
Then, with joy I'll car - ry on, Until the
L
ten.
ten.
day my eyes be-hold the cit - y
f
Un - til the
Broaden
day God calls me home.

SPRINGS OF LIVING WATER

HAMMOND	SPINET	OTHERS
(U) – 00 8080 800	(U) – 00 8080 800	(U) – Clarinet 8', Flute 2'–$2\frac{2}{3}$'
[L] – [F]	[L] – 5543 2222	[L] – Strings & Flutes 8'
Ped.– 54	Ped.– 4 or 5	Ped.– Bourdon 16', Flute 8'
Full Vibrato	Full Vibrato	Full Vibrato

JOHN W. PETERSON
Arr. by Fred Bock

Brightly

* Observe right hand phrase markings very carefully.

f
mf
mp
f
L
mp
sfz p

AM I A SOLDIER OF THE CROSS?

Arr. by
FRED BOCK

Steadily

Add
mf Flute 8', 4',
(tremolo)
mf
rit.
Sw. 4' Flute, tremolo
Gt. reduce to
l. h. Strings alone
a tempo

Sw. Light reed
mf
Gt.
mp
ritard.
pp

TO BE FREE

HAMMOND
(U)pper: (B) 06 3804 370 Vibrato off
Percussion on, normal, fast, second
[L]ower: [F] or 00 5543 222 Vibrato off
Pedal: 52

OTHERS
(U)pper: Flutes 4', 5 1/3', 2 2/3', 2'
Percussion on, fast decay
[L]ower: Strings 8', Flutes 8', 4'
Pedal: String bass effect 8', or 16'

Words and Music by
EDDIE SMITH
Arr. by Fred Bock

sion, Dis - con - tent, dis - il - lu - sion, Do you
A9 Em A9
have what it takes to be free? Are you
Em C F♯m7/B
free from dis - as - ter? Do you know what you're af - ter? Do you
Em9 A9 Em9 A9
have what it takes to be free?
C Bm Am G F Em A9

mf
There's a life that's worth liv - ing; There's a
Em A9 Em A9
way of for-giv - ing All your sin, guilt, and trou - ble, you
Em A9 Em C
see. Just let Christ be your Mas -
F#m/B Em9
ter; Then you'll find what you're af - ter, And you'll
A9 Em9 A9

have what it takes to be free. To be
C Bm Am G F A9
Smoothly
vibrato on
mf
free, to be free, Do you
Am D9 G maj7 C
have what it takes to be free?
G F7 F♯m7/B
Are you
vibrato off
free from dis - as - ter? Do you
Em9 A9

Broaden
know what you're af - ter? Do you have what it
Em9 A9 Cmaj7 Bm7 Am7
takes to be free?
a tempo
G maj7 F Em A9
Em A9 Em
mp
A9 Em

SWING LOW, SWEET CHARIOT

HAMMOND	SPINET	OTHERS
Upper: 00 6050 200 Full Vibrato	Upper: 00 6050 200 Full Vibrato	Upper: Clarinet 8' Tremolo
Lower: 00 5432 110 Full Vibrato	Lower: 5432 1100 Full Vibrato	Lower: Soft Flute & Strg. 8'
Pedal: 43	Pedal: 4	Pedal: Bourdon 16'

Traditional Spiritual
Arr. by Fred Bock

a little faster
com - in' for to car - ry me home. I
looked o - ver Jor - dan and what did I see
com - in' for to car - ry me
home? A band of an - gels com - in' af - ter me
rit.
Com - in' for to car - ry me home.
fp
p

IT TOOK A MIRACLE

HAMMOND ORGANS

Upper: 60 5755 000
Lower: 00 5253 001
Pedal: 42
Full Vibrato

ALL ORGANS

Upper: Strings 16′,8′
Soft Reed 8′
Lower: Open Diapason 8′
Pedal: Bourdon 16′, 8′
Full Vibrato

Arranged by
FRED BOCK

Words and Music by
JOHN W. PETERSON

ten.
mir-a-cle to put the stars in place, It took a mir-a-cle to hang the
Eb
Bb7
world in space. But when He saved my soul, cleansed and made me
ten.
ten.
ten.
Fm B Eb
C7 Gm(b5) C7 Fm7
Bb G aug. G7
a little faster
whole, It took a mir-a-cle
Cm
F7
E
rit.
ten.
a tempo
ff
It took a mir-a-cle to put the
Abm
Gm C7
F Ab dim.

Broaden
ten.
stars in place. It took a mir-a-cle to hang the world in space. But when He
Gm C7 Eb7 Gm C7 Ab dim. F6
saved my soul, cleansed and made me
D7 Gm C7 A7
whole. It took a mir-a-cle of love and grace.
Faster
Dm G7 Gm C7 F
rit.
p
Gb Ab Bb Eb F

AMAZING GRACE

HAMMOND ORGANS

Upper: 00 8282 650
Lower: 00 6734 121
Pedal: 40
Full Vibrato

ALL ORGANS

Upper: Clarinet 8′, Flutes 22/3′, 2′
Lower: Soft Strings 8′, 4′
Pedal: Bourdon 16′
Full Vibrato

Arranged by
FRED BOCK

AMERICAN FOLK MELODY
Words by JOHN NEWTON

Moderato, *with feeling*

now I see. Through man - y dan - gers,
Dsus. D7 G C D7 G B7
toils, and snares I have al - read - y come; 'Tis grace hath brought me safe thus far, And
C D7 G D7 G C A7 Dsus.
D7 G G7 C G
grace will lead me home. When
C A7 D sus. D7 G G sus. G7

A little faster
f
we've been there ten thou - sand years, bright shin - ing as the sun; We've no less days to sing God's praise than when we first be - gun.
ritard
C E7 F G7 C G
Am D7 G9 G7
C Gm C7 F B7 B♭ A Fm C
G sus. G7 C Fm C

THE BROKEN VESSEL

HAMMOND ORGANS

Upper: A# 01 6008 334
Lower: B 00 5523 222
Pedal: 50
Full Vibrato

OTHER ORGANS

Upper: Clarinet 8', Flute 2'
Lower: Gamba, on String 8'
Pedal: Light Flute 16'
Full Vibrato

Arr. by Fred Bock

Words and Music by
ANDRAÉ CROUCH

so much com - pas - sion to make it o - ver a -
gain. Oh! I was that ves - sel
that no one thought was good, I cried
f
"Lord, you're the Pot - ter and I am the clay, Make me o - ver a -

gain to - day". Then God picked up the
piec - es of my bro - ken heart that day.
Then He made me a new ves - sel And re -
On 16'
vived my soul a - gain.
rit. to end
f

16

BATTLE HYMN OF THE REPUBLIC

JULIA WARD HOWE
(Adapted from an arrangement by Roy Ringwald)

HAMMOND:
(G♯)
[A♯] 23 7888 556
Ped. 50

OTHERS:
(Sw.) Trumpet 8'
Sw. to Sw. 4'
[Gt.] Open Diapason 8'
Octave 4', Fifteenth 2'
Ped. Open Diapason 16'
Flute 8'

Gt.
(Optional)
add 8'
(Hammond 55 or 66)
In tempo
Gt.
mf
Add Tremolo
Vib. 2
ten.
f
mp
l.h.
pp
Gt.

Ad lib.
ten.
Broaden
ten.
ten.
Off Tremolo
and Vibrato
ff
Add sfz
rit.

JUST A CLOSER WALK WITH THEE

HAMMOND ORGANS

Upper: 60 3736 000
Lower: 00 5532 200
Pedal: 53
Small Vibrato

ALL ORGANS

Upper: Strings 16′, 8′, Flutes 8′, 2′
Lower: Diapason 8′
Pedal: Medium Loud 16′, 8′
Small Vibrato

Arranged by
FRED BOCK

SPIRITUAL

Dai - ly walk-ing close to Thee
Dm7 G7 D♭9 C C7 F
Let it be, dear Lord, let it be.
D7 sus. D7 C Am Dm Gsus. G7 C Am
Dm7 G7 D♭6 C Am Dm7 G7 D♭6 C
I am
weak, but Thou art strong Je - - sus,
Em E♭m Dm G7 G7 sus.

keep me from all wrong.
G7 Gsus. C A7 Dm G7
I'll be sat - is - fied as long
C C7 F
as I walk, dear Lord, close to
slower
D7sus. D7 C Am Dm D♭
a tempo
Thee.
mf rit. mp
C A7/C♮ Fm C

NOW I BELONG TO JESUS

HAMMOND	SPINET	OTHERS
Upper: 00 8281 400	Upper: 00 8281 400	Upper: Clarinet 8'
Lower: [F] or [F#]	Lower: 5605 2211	Lower: Strings 8', 4'
Pedal: 41	Pedal: 4	Pedal: Bourdon 16'
Full Vibrato	Full Vibrato	Full Vibrato

NORMAN CLAYTON
Arr. by Fred Bock

Tenderly, with feeling

U
NOW I BE - LONG TO JE - SUS,
U
L
Je - sus be-longs to me,
Not for the years of time a - lone,
But for e - ter - ni - ty.
Faster
mf
Ab
Bbm Cm Bbm
Cm Bbm
Bbm Eb7
Ab
Ebm6 F7
Db D°
Ab Eb7
Ab
F G7
Gm C7

a tempo
E♭ F7 D♭ E♭7 A♭
B♭m E♭7 B♭m E♭7 A♭
E♭m6 F7 D♭ D° A♭ D♭
Faster
rit.
E♭7 E C♯m6 F♯7 A♭

GREAT IS THY FAITHFULNESS

HAMMOND	SPINET	OTHERS
Upper: (A#) 00 7817 224 Vibrato 3	Upper: 00 7817 224 Full Vibrato	Upper: Flutes 8', 4', 2' Vibrato
Lower: [A#] 005523 201 Vibrato 3	Lower: 5523 2000 Full Vibrato	Lower: Flutes & Strings 8', 4' Vibrato
Pedal: 42	Pedal: 4	Pedal: Bourdon 16' Soft String 16'

WILLIAM RUNYAN
Arr. by Fred Bock

ten.
a tempo
GREAT IS THY
Gm7 C7 F Db
FAITH - FUL - NESS, O God, my Fa - ther. There is no shad - ow of
Gb Ab7 Db Gb Gb7 Db Bb7
turn - ing with Thee; L Thou chang-est not Thy com - pas - sions they
f
Eb7 Ab7(4-3) Ab7 F7 Bbm Gb Fm7 Bb7
fail not; As Thou hast been Thou for - ev - er wilt be.
ten.
U
f
ten.
Ebm G° Db(Ab bass) Gbmaj7 (Ab bass) Ab7 Db

GREAT IS THY FAITH-FUL-NESS, GREAT IS THY FAITH-FUL-NESS!
C7 F Am D7 Gm
Morn-ing by morn-ing new mer-cies I see. L All I have
C7 A7 Dm Fm6 C G7 C7 A7
need - ed Thy hand hath pro-vid-ed GREAT IS THY FAITH-FUL-NESS,
Dm B♭7 Am7 D9 Gm7 E7 F
Very broadly
Lord, un-to me!
Gm7 C7 F Gm7 D♭ G♭ F

I JUST FEEL LIKE SOMETHING GOOD IS ABOUT TO HAPPEN

Hammond Organ
Upper: A♯ 03 7886 644
Lower: A♯ 00 6746 324
Pedal: 63

Other Organs
Upper: Full Ensemble, no 16′, Flutes, Strings, Diapasons (no reeds, except very light) 8′, 4′, 2′
Lower: Diapasons 4′, Strings & Flutes 8′, 4′
Pedal: Bourdon 16′, Flute 16′, 8′

Words and Music by
WILLIAM J. GAITHER

Strongly, but not slowly

way; He has prom-ised that He'd o - pen all of
heav - en, And broth - er it could hap-pen an - y
day. When God's peo-ple hum-ble them - selves to call on
Je - sus, And they look to Heav - en ex - pect - ing as they

pray; I just feel like some-thing good is a-bout to
hap - pen, And broth-er, this could be that ver-y
day!

IN THE GARDEN

HAMMOND	SPINET	OTHERS
Upper: 00 6050 200 Full Vibrato	Upper: 00 6050 200 Full Vibrato	Upper: Clarinet 8' Tremolo
Lower: 00 5432 110 Full Vibrato	Lower: 5432 1100 Full Vibrato	Lower: Soft Flute & Strg. 8'
Pedal: 43	Pedal: 4	Pedal: Bourdon 16'

Arranged by
FRED BOCK

C. AUSTIN MILES

A♭ B♭7 E♭7
hear, fall-ing on my ear the Son of God dis - clos -
A♭ E♭
- es. And___ He walks with me, and He talks with
ten.
ten.
B♭m7 E♭7 A♭
me, and He tells me I am His own.______ And the
A♭ C7 Fm A♭7 D♭ A♭
joy we share as we tar - ry there none oth - er has

A little faster
E♭7 Ab E♭7 Ab C7 Fm Ab7 D♭ G♭7 Ab E♭7 Ab
ev - er known. And He walks with me, and He talks with me, and He tells me I am His own. And the joy we share as we tar - ry there none oth - er has ev - er known.
mf
ten.
L
pp

IN TIMES LIKE THESE

HAMMOND	SPINET	OTHERS
Upper: (D#) or (F#) Vibrato 3	Upper: 00 8260 000 Vibrato	Upper: Flutes 8', 4', 2' Full Vibrato
Lower: [F] Vibrato 3	Lower: 0046 3400 Vibrato	Lower: Soft Strings 8', 4' Flutes 8', 4'
Pedal: 52	Pedal: 5	Pedal: Bourdon 16' Soft Flute 8'

RUTH CAYE JONES
Arr. by Fred Bock

Warmly, with much feeling

an - chor; Be ver - y sure, be ver - y sure your an - chor
Bb F Bb
holds and grips the sol - id rock! L This rock is
ten.
F C7 F
Je - sus, Yes, He's the One; This rock is Je - sus, The on - ly
C7 F C7
U
One. Be ver - y sure, be ver - y sure your an - chor
F Bb

holds ___ and grips the sol - id rock! ___
L
f
F
C7
F
ten.
f
ten.
U
mp
ten.
f
ten.
A♭7
D♭
C7 (E bass)
E♭m
A♭7
D♭
ten.
ten. ten.
F7(♭9)
G♭
G°
D♭ (A♭ bass)
ten.
E♭m7
A♭7
rit.
mp
tr
pppp
D♭
G♭
D♭

HE IS THE WAY, HE IS THE TRUTH, HE IS THE LIFE

HAMMOND		OTHERS	
(U)pper:	(A#) 00 4682 411 or F No Vibrato	(U)pper:	Oboe or Trumpet 8' No Vibrato
Prepare:	(B) 00 6802 000	Prepare:	Flute Chorus 8', 4',2'
[L]ower:	[A#] 00 5433 111 no Vibrato	[L]ower:	Strings and Flutes 8', 4' no Vibrato
Prepare:	[B] 00 7845 335	Prepare:	Full Ensemble, no 16', no Reeds
Pedal:	54	Pedal:	Flutes 16', 8', Gt. to Ped.

Words and Music by
OTIS SKILLINGS
Arr. by Fred Bock

Bright, fast and happy (in 2)
(U) (A#) (Reed)

He is the Way; He is the Truth; He is the
Life.
B♭m F Dm Gm C7
F Gm/C F F Gm/C F
3
F A7 Dm F7 B♭ E♭/F B♭
F Gm Am Gm C7 F Gm/F F

F A7 Dm B♭m F Dm Gm C7
Slower (in 4) with a light blues feel, heavily accented
B
Full vibrato on
(Flutes)
U
rit.
F Gm/F F B♭7 F9 B♭7 F7
B♭7 F7 B♭7 F7 B♭7 E♭9 E9 E♭7
B♭9 E♭9 B♭9 E♭9 B♭7 F9 B♭9 F7

B♭ D7 Gm E♭m B♭ Gm C7 F7
B♭7 E♭ B♭7 E♭ B♭ B♭7 E♭
L
B♭7 E♭ B♭ B♭7 F9 B♭7 F7
U
B♭7 F7 B♭7 E9 E♭9 E9 E♭9

B♭7
E♭9
B♭7
E♭9
B♭7
E♭9
B♭7
F9
B♭7
E♭9
D7(sus)
D7(♭5)
Gm
E♭m
B♭
Gm
C9
F7
rit.
Vibrato off
a tempo
accelerando
L (Full, B)
B♭
Fast again, as in the beginning (in 2)
ala Baroque style.
U
Registration:
Hammond: Change B to 00 6002 008
Others: Flutes 8', 2' only
E♭
A♭
Fm
E♭
E♭
G7
Cm
A♭
E♭

Fm F♯o E♭ A♭ B♭(sus) E♭ A♭ E♭ Fm
E♭ G7 Cm A♭m E♭ G7
L
Broaden
U
L
f
Cm E♭ E♭7 A♭ Am(♭5) E♭ B♭(sus)
ff
fff
B♭7 E♭ D♭7/E♭ E♭

HAVE YOU ANY ROOM FOR JESUS?

HAMMOND	OTHERS
Upper A# 02 8558 444	Upper Flutes 8', 4', 2⅔', 2'
Lower A# 00 5817 211	Lower Strings 8', 4'
Ped. 52	Flute 8'
Full Vibrato	Ped. Flutes 16', 8'
	Full Vibrato

Words & Music by
C. C. Williams
Arranged by Fred Bock

1
bey;
Swing your heart's door wide-ly o - pen,
Bid Him en-ter while you may.
D.C.
2
bey.
f
Swing your heart's door wide-ly o - pen,
rit.
Bid Him en-ter while you may.
a bit faster
f
Vibrato off
Lower
pp

ALL HE WANTS IS YOU

HAMMOND ORGANS

Upper: A♯ 00 80807 000
Lower: F♯ preset
Pedal: 51
Full Vibrato

OTHER ORGANS

Upper: Oboe 8', Flute 4'
Lower: Soft Flutes 8', 4'
Pedal: Flute 16', 8'
Full Vibrato

Arr. by Fred Bock

Words and Music by
AUDREY MIEIR

not just a part, He wants all of your
heart; All He wants is all of you,
All He wants is you.
Upper
mp Some-thing more than gold for the Mas - ter,

Some-thing more than gifts to ap - pease. There is
on - ly one thing that you a - lone can bring; there is
on - ly one gift that will please.
mf
Lower

Upper
accel.
rit.
f
Lower
mf

CONSTANTLY ABIDING

HAMMOND
Ⓤpper: Ⓐ♯ 00 8080 800
Ⓛower: Ⓐ♯ 00 5433 110
Pedal: 42
Full vibrato

OTHERS
Ⓤpper: Clarinet 8'
Ⓛower: Strings 8', 4'
Pedal: Light Flute 16'
Full vibrato

Words and Music by
Mrs. WILL MURPHY
Arr. by Fred Bock

cloud, I've a peace that has come there to stay!
G maj7 D E7 D Bm Dm A E A7(sus)
A7
In a light, easy tempo
D
Con - stant-ly a - bid - ing, Je - sus is mine.
A7
Con - stant-ly a - bid - ing, rap - ture di -
Em E♭9

vine! He nev - er leaves me lone - ly,
D
Whis - pers, oh, so kind: "I will nev - er leave thee."
Am D7 G Bm E7 D B7
Je - sus is mine.
f
Em A7 D
A7

Em E♭9 D
7
f
Am D7
G Bm E7 D B7 Em A7
mp
D B♭ D

EVERY TIME I FEEL THE SPIRIT

HAMMOND	SPINET	OTHERS
Upper: Ⓐ♯ 00 8888 444 No Vibrato	Upper: 00 8888 444 No Vibrato	Upper: Trumpet 8' No Vibrato
Lower: G	Lower: 5654 4442 Full Vibrato	Lower: Full Organ 8', 4', 2' Full Vibrato
Pedal: 55	Pedal: 5	Pedal: Heavy 16' & 8'

SPIRITUAL
Arr. by Fred Bock

To Coda
SPIR - IT, mov - in' in my heart I — will pray. — Up-on the moun-tain my Lord
spoke, From His mouth came fire — and smoke! The Jor-dan riv - er, it's so
D. S. al Coda CODA
cold, chills the bod - y, not — the soul. EV-'RY pray. —
L

U
f
Very broadly
ff
ff

COME, HOLY SPIRIT

HAMMOND
Upper: 02 8876 331
Full Vibrato
Lower: F
Full Vibrato
Pedal: 54

SPINET
Upper: 02 8876 331
Full Vibrato
Lower: 6534 2100
Full Vibrato
Pedal: 5

OTHERS
Upper: Full Swell (Except 5 1/3' & 16', Full Vibrato
Lower: Strings & Flute 8'
Diapason 8', Full Vibrato
Pedal: Gt. to Ped. 8'
Bourdon 16'

Words by
WILLIAM GAITHER
and GLORIA GAITHER

Music by
WILLIAM GAITHER
Arr. by Fred Bock

Take me: soul, bo - dy and mind.
COME, HO - LY SPIR - IT, I need Thee,
Come, sweet Spir - it, I pray.
Come, in Thy strength and Thy pow - er,
Come, in Thy own gen - tle way.

A little faster
L
mp
U
mf
ten.
ten.
f
ten.
L
mp
pp

HE'S GOT THE WHOLE WORLD IN HIS HANDS

HAMMOND ORGANS

Upper: 00 6824 100 - Full Vibrato
Lower: 00 5624 200 - No Vibrato
Pedal: 52

ALL ORGANS

Upper: Tibias 8', 4', 2', String 4' - Full Vibrato
Lower: Flute 8', Tibia Clausa 4'- No Vibrato
Pedal: String bass effect 16', 8'

Arranged by
FRED BOCK

SPIRITUAL

Tenderly
mp
whole world in His hands. He's got the
lit-tle tin-y ba-by in His hands, He's got the
Am D7 G C
lit-tle tin-y ba-by in His hands, He's got the lit-tle tin-y ba-by in His hands, He's got the
Dm G7 C F C
Brightly
f
whole world in His hands. He's got the wind and rain in His hands, He's got the
Dm G7 C A♭7 D♭
wind and rain in His hands, He's got the wind and rain
E♭m A♭7 D♭

in His hands, He's got the whole world in His hands. He's got the
D♭ E♭m D♭ A7
Broaden
whole world in His hands, He's got the whole world
D Bm D Bm D Bm D Bm Em A7
Smoothly
in His hands, He's got the whole world in His hands, He's got the whole world
D Bm D Bm D G D Em
in His hands.
Em A7 D G B♭+ D
ff

THE SPIRIT OF JESUS IS IN THIS PLACE

Hammond Organ
UPPER: A♯ 00 5670 000
LOWER: A♯ 00 4314 000
PEDAL: 42
Full Vibrato

other Organs
UPPER: Flutes 8′, 4′, 2⅔′
LOWER: Strings 8′, 4′
PEDAL: Gedeckt 16′
Full Vibrato

Words by
GLORIA & WILLIAM J. GAITHER

Music by
WILLIAM J. GAITHER
Arr. Fred Bock

face When the pow'r of Heav'n is
tapped, then, Some-thing good is bound to hap-pen, for the
white note gliss.
Spir-it of Je-sus is in this place.
2nd time only, both hands on Lower
(2nd ×)
Fine
mp
f
Upper
Oh, my friend He is so near that we could touch Him

His sweet pres - ence this ole' world could ne'er re - place
Won't you let His Spir - it warm you let His might - y love trans - form you while the Spir - it of Je - sus is in this place.
Lower
white note gliss.
8va
f
loco
D. S. al fine
Upper
mf

THOU DIDST LEAVE THY THRONE

HAMMOND		PIPE and ELECTRONIC	
Sw.:	(A#) 00 8040 000	Sw.:	Flute solo, 4' Tremolo
Gt.:	[E] or [F#] Vibrato 2	Gt.:	Strings 8', String Celeste 8'
Ped.:	51	Ped.:	Light 16'

Timothy R. Matthews
Arr. by Fred Bock

a little faster
Sw.
mf
ten.
ten.
mf
(♯)
Gt.
mf

ten.
ten.
R.H.
L.H.
pp
Soft 32'

TEACH ME, LORD, TO WAIT

HAMMOND	SPINET	OTHERS
Upper: G♯ Full Vibrato	Upper: 03 8866 221 Full Vibrato	Upper: Trumpette 8', 4' Full Vibrato
Lower: F♯ Full Vibrato	Lower: 4444 3311 Full Vibrato	Lower: Strings 8', 4', Flute 8' Full Vibrato
Pedal: 54	Pedal: 5	Pedal: Flute 8', Strings 16'

STUART HAMBLEN

Arr. by Fred Bock

ly on what oth - ers do, But to wait in pray - er for an
an - swer from You. "They that wait up-on the Lord shall re - new their
strength; U They shall mount up with wings as ea - gles; —
— They shall run, and not be wea-ry; They shall walk, and not faint," Teach me,
3
3
L

rubato
ten. ten.
Lord, Teach me, Lord, To Wait.
L
ten.
ten.
U
a tempo
f
L
rit.

THE LORD IS COUNTING ON YOU

HAMMOND	SPINET	OTHERS
Upper: 02 8846 002 Full Vibrato	Upper: 02 8846 002 Full Vibrato	Upper: Flutes 8',4',2' Full Vibrato
Lower: F Full Vibrato	Lower: 4523 2000 Full Vibrato	Lower: 8', 4' Full Vibrato
Pedal: 53	Pedal: 5	Pedal: Bourdon 16', Soft Flute 8'

STUART HAMBLEN
Arr. by Fred Bock

Talk just a lit-tle bit, sing just a lit-tle bit, throw in a smile or
two, But heav-y on the "How-dy - do." For the
Lord is a-count-ing on, Lord is a-count-ing on, Lord is a-count-ing on
ten.
Brightly
you. I love to go to Sun - day School, I love to sing the
ten.
ten.

songs. I hate to see a va-cant pew, I know there's some-thing
Smoothly
wrong. I want the Lord to be proud of me, His work I'll glad-ly
do. I know a song to get them in, Just list-en and learn it
f
too.
7

ff

IVORY PALACES

Suggested Registration
For General Electronic or Pipe Organs
Upper: Flutes 16', 8', 4', 2'
Lower: Strings 8,
French Horn 8'
Pedal: 16', 8', Medium

Suggested Registration
For Pre-Set Organs
(A#) 60 7806 000
(B) 80 0800 000
[A#] 00 5505 000
Pedal 5-3
Vibrato 3

Suggested Registration
For Spinet Drawbar Organs
(U) 60 7806 000
[L] 5505 0000
Pedal 3
Vibrato On, Normal

HENRY BARRACLOUGH
Arranged by Fred Bock

In - to a world of woe.
On - ly His great e - ter - nal love
ten.
made my Sav - ior go.
ten.
ten.
Faster
L
My
Lord has gar - ments so won - drous fine, And

myrrh their tex - ture fills; It's fra - grance
reached to this heart of mine, With joy my
be - ing thrills.
U
In tempo as in the beginning
L
(♭)

Accented
ff
ten.
ten.
ff
ten.
ten.
mp
U
Slowly
L

THIS OLE HOUSE

HAMMOND
Upper: 00 8888 444
Full Vibrato
Lower: F
Full Vibrato
Pedal: 55

SPINET
Upper: 00 8888 444
Full Vibrato
Lower: 5535 2300
Full Vibrato
Pedal: 6

OTHERS
Upper: Flutes & Strings 8',4',2'
Full Vibrato
Lower: Diapason 8'
Full Vibrato
Pedal: Bourdon 16',Flute & Strings 8'

STUART HAMBLEN
Arr. by Fred Bock

shouts, Now she trem-bles in the dark-ness When the light-nin' walks a -
bout. Well, I ain't a - gon - na need this house no long - er, Ain't a - gon - na
need this house no more, Ain't got time to fix the shin - gles, Ain't got
time to fix the floor, Ain't got time to oil the hing - es Nor to

mend the win - dow panes. Ain't a - gon - na need this house no
long - er, I'm a - get - tin' read - y to meet the saints.
Add 16' to Upper (80 8888 444)
ff

Presto
ff
mf
ff

SOMETHING BEAUTIFUL

HAMMOND
Upper: 00 8004 002
Lower: 00 6524 002
Pedal: 52
Full Vibrato

OTHERS
Upper: Flutes 8', 2'
Lower: Flutes & Strings 8'
Pedal: Gedeckt 16'
Full Vibrato

Words by GLORIA GAITHER

Music by WILLIAM J. GAITHER
Arr. by Fred Bock

All my con - fu - sion,
He un - der - stood;
All I had to of - fer Him was
bro - ken - ness and strife, but He made some - thing
beau - ti - ful of my life.
ten.
ten.
ten.
If there
Lower

ad lib.
ev - er were dreams that were loft - y and no - ble,
they were my dreams at the
start;
and the hopes for life's best were the hopes that I har - bored.
Down deep in my heart;
Upper
But my dreams turned to ash - es, my
cas - tles all crumbled, my for - tune turned to loss,
So I
Lower

wrapped it all in the rags of my life, and laid it at the
cross.
Upper

Lower
ten.
pp

BEYOND THE SUNSET

HAMMOND	SPINET	OTHERS
Upper: 00 8007 000 Full Vibrato	Upper: 00 8007 000 Full Vibrato	Upper: Flutes 8' 2' Tremolo
Lower: F♯ Full Vibrato	Lower: 6533 2100 Full Vibrato	Lower: Flutes & String 8'
Pedal: 44	Pedal: 4	Pedal: Bourdon 16' Soft 8'

Arranged by
FRED BOCK

BLANCHE BROCK
VIRGIL BROCK

G7
Ab
end - ed, O glo - rious dawn - ing,
D7
Eb
Fm
Bb7
ten.
Be - yond the sun - set, when day is
ten.
ten.
Eb
done. Be - yond the sun - set,
Fm
Bb7
no clouds will gath - er no storms will

Fm
Bb7
Eb
threat - en, no fears at all.
D7
Eb
G+
O day of glad - ness, O day un -
Ab
A°
Eb
end - ing, Be - yond the sun - set,
Fm
Bb7
Eb
F7
Eb
ten. ad lib.
e - ter - nal joy.
ten.
ten.

THE OLD RUGGED CROSS

HAMMOND	SPINET	OTHERS
Upper: 00 8807 002 Full Vibrato	Upper: 00 8807 002 Full Vibrato	Upper: Flutes 8' 4' 2' Tremolo
Lower: 00 4533 220 Full Vibrato	Lower: 4533 2200 Full Vibrato	Lower: Strings 8' 4'
Pedal: 43	Pedal: 4	Pedal: Bourdon 16'

Arranged by
FRED BOCK

GEORGE BERNARD

G U Am D7 G
slain. So I'll cher - ish the old rug - ged cross,
C G
'Til my tro - phies at last I lay down; I will
G C G C G
cling to the old rug - ged cross, And ex - change it some
D7 B♭m
day for a crown. So, I'll cher - ish the

E♭ A♭ D7 D♭
old rug - ged cross, 'Till my tro - phies at
A little slower
A♭ F7
last I lay down; I will cling to the
D♭ F7 B♭m G♭7 A♭
old rug - ged cross, And ex - change it some
E♭7 A♭ E♮ A♭
ten.
day for a crown.
ten.
ten.
pp

HOLY HANDS

HAMMOND	SPINET	OTHERS
Upper: D♯ Full Vibrato	Upper: 00 8800 000 Full Vibrato	Upper: French Horn 8' Full Vibrato
Lower: F♯ Full Vibrato	Lower: 4430 2200 Full Vibrato	Lower: Soft Strings 8', 4' Full Vibrato
Pedal: 43	Pedal: 5	Pedal: Bourdon 16'

CARL FARRER

Arr. by Fred Bock

With great warmth and feeling

ten. ten. ten.
would be mend - ed by His hand And oh His
eyes that look at me And HO - LY
HANDS that ten - der - ly e - rase the trou - ble from my
ten.
brow ten. Oh I can al - most feel them
ten.

ten. ten. ten.
now L And oh His eyes that look at
ten.
me And Ho-ly Hands that ten-der-ly e-rase the
p
ten.
trou-ble from my brow O I can al-most feel them
Very soft flute stop D♯
U
8va
ten.
now O Ho-ly Hands, O Ho-ly Hands.

THE OLD RUGGED CROSS MADE THE DIFFERENCE

HAMMOND		OTHERS	
Upper:	00 8870 000	Upper:	Clarinet 8'
Lower:	(F♯) or 00 5642 112	Lower:	Strings & Flutes 8', 4'
Pedal:	41	Pedal:	Gedeckt 16'
Full Vibrato		Full Vibrato	

Words by WILLIAM J. GAITHER
and GLORIA GAITHER

Music by WILLIAM J. GAITHER
Arr. by Fred Bock

Just one touch, then a new life be - gan. And the
old Rug-ged Cross made the dif-f'rence in a life bound for
heart-ache and de - feat; I will praise Him for - ev - er, and
ev - er, for the cross made the diff - 'rence for me.

a little faster
f
Lower
rit.

BORN AGAIN

HAMMOND

Ⓤpper: Ⓐ♯ 00 3805 000
Vibrato 1
Prepare: Ⓑ 04 4805 002
[L]ower: [F] or 00 4423 111
Vibrato off
Pedal: 43

OTHERS

Ⓤpper: Flutes 4', 2' String 8'
Small Vibrato
[L]ower: Dulciana 8', Gemshorn 8'
Vibrato off
Pedal: Bourdon 16'

Words and Music by
OTIS SKILLINGS
Arr. by Fred Bock

had a song to sing. Yet one day that bird will fly Far a-way up in the sky. So our lives once came to be. We can think and we can see; Yet be-yond there's even more If we'll just un-lock the door. There's a
Fm7 F7(sus) F7 B♭m7 Gm7(♭5)
Fm C7(sus) C7 Fm B♭7 D♭ Fm B♭m7 E♭9 A♭maj7 D♭maj7
Gm7(♭5) C7 F maj7 F6 B♭m7 E♭9
A♭maj7 D♭maj7 Gm7(♭5) C7 F maj7 F6
Vibrato on, Add 8' Flute
Smoothly
Hammond: 04 4805 002
ten.
(registration like the beginning)

new world to be found, And a great life to a-
Fm7
Gm7(♭5)
bound. Like the flow'r be-neath the rain, So can
Fm7
F7(sus)
F7
B♭m7
Gm7(♭5)
we be born a - gain, be born a - gain; be born a - gain, be born a-
Fm
C7(sus)
C7
Fm
B♭7
Fm
B♭7
Fm
B♭9
ritard
gain, be born a - gain!
mp
p
pp
G♭
F maj9

NO MORE

HAMMOND

Upper: 00 8800 200
Full Vibrato

Lower: F♯
Full Vibrato

Pedal: 44

SPINET

Upper: 00 8800 200
Full Vibrato

Lower: 4513 2222
Full Vibrato

Pedal: 4

OTHERS

Upper: Flute 8' (mf)
Full Vibrato

Lower: Salicional 8', 4', 2'
Full Vibrato

Pedal: Bourdon 16'

AUDREY MIEIR
Arr. by Fred Bock

Warmly

plead with you. No MORE, No
MORE as He's done be - fore. Your wait - ing
U
time is through. You've wast - ed the
past and now at last you're fac - ing the

end of to - day. There's no hu - man
force can change your course, there's no oth - er
way but to pray. L Once more, once
more, as He's done be fore, He may call once

more for you Once more, once
more He may knock at the door. Then no more will He
plead with you.
U
L pp
ppp

BLESSED ASSURANCE

Suggested Registration
For General Electronic or Pipe Organs

Upper: Strings 16', 8'
Reed 8'
Lower: Open Diapason 8'
Pedal: Bourdon 16', 8'

Suggested Registration
For Pre-Set Organs

(A#) 60 5755 000
[A#] 00 5525 000
Pedal 5–2
Vibrato 2

Suggested Registration
For Spinet Drawbar Organs

(U) 60 5755 000
[L] 5525 0000
Pedal 3
Vibrato On, Normal

FANNY CROSBY

Mrs. JOSEPH KNAPP
Arranged by Fred Bock

long! This is my sto - ry, this is my song, Prais-ing my Sav-ior all the day
long. This is my sto - ry this is my song. Prais-ing my
Broaden
f
a tempo
Sav - ior all the day long.
Very slowly and softly
ten.
L
p

THE LOVE OF GOD

HAMMOND	SPINET	OTHERS
Upper: 00 8857 002	Upper: 00 8857 002	Upper: Flutes 8', 4', 2', 2 2/3'
Lower: [F♯] or [F]	Lower: 5542 0010	Lower: Strings 8', 4'
Pedal: 43 Full Vibrato	Pedal: 4 Full Vibrato	Pedal: Soft 16', 8' Full Vibrato

F. M. LEHMAN
Arr. by Fred Bock

pure, how meas-ure - less and strong. It shall for-
Eb Cm Fm Bb7 Eb
ev - er-more en - dure the saint's and an - gels'
Ab Ab7 Eb Cm Fm Bb7
ten. A little faster
song.
Eb C G7
C Am Dm G7 C G7 C G7

mf
L
ten. ten. ten.
ten. ten. ten.
C Am Dm G7 C C7 F Fm B♭7
U
C Am Dm G7 C E7 F Fm B7
ten. Broaden
ten.
C Am Dm G7 C C B♭
ten.
a tempo
mp
Fm A♭ D♭9 E♭9 C